# TIPS

# FOR READING

# PEOPLE LIKE BOOKS

## Using Body Language to Figure Out What They Feel

By

## MARCI R. VAUGHN

# Disclaimer

No part of this book may be reproduced or transmitted in any form or by any means, electronic or mechanical, including photocopying, recording or by any information storage and retrieval system, without written permission from the author."

# Table of Contents

# Introduction

Reading people's body language, also known as reading non-verbal cues, is a means to conclude the individuals you interact with or see in your environment. Reading someone's body language is a skill that, if mastered, may reveal a great deal about that person's emotions, mental state, or what they truly mean while they are speaking (this is particularly true in situations in which the person is lying).

When you train yourself to be more aware of your surroundings, you'll notice more of them automatically, which will help you stay safer. assist you in picking up on clues from body language. However, keep a low profile and watch discreetly so that your actions won't influence how others behave. The process of becoming familiar with the "baseline" behavior of a person Every person has idiosyncrasies and routines that are unique to them. If you are familiar with their typical behavior, you will be better able to notice when they are engaging in strange behavior, allowing you to determine whether or not anything is wrong and take appropriate action.

# Chapter 1

## Body Language: Becoming an expert reader of body language.

Becoming an expert reader of body language requires first understanding what body language is. Body language is a subset of non-verbal communication that emphasizes the use of gestures, poses, and other physical cues as a means of information exchange rather than the use of words. You will be able to better understand the feelings and states of mind of other people if you are skilled at reading the indicators of body language. This helps you grasp what they really believe or how they truly feel about a certain topic. After that, you will be able to answer them suitably.

Body language may be affected by a variety of factors, including cultural standards and developmental difficulties, for instance, if you always think that individuals who avoid eye contact are dishonest, you are likely to incorrectly assess a large number of completely trustworthy people. If you are a neurotypical person engaging with a neurodiverse person, such as an autistic person, the phrase "trusting your instincts" may not function as well as you want it to. Before drawing any conclusions, be sure you have considered all of the available evidence. It is easy to misinterpret a little detail, so it is important to check for more than one indicator. Don't get into anything too quickly, do not be hesitant to inquire of others as to how they are doing. It is possible to have a better understanding of the other person and perhaps grow closer to them if you ask them questions. You should encourage others to share with you what is going on in their lives.

You have to train yourself to be aware of the context around you. To be a good observer, this requires you to maintain a vigilant awareness of your whereabouts and the activities occurring in your immediate environment at all times. Be aware that there are regional variations in body language. Here are some more suggestions that can assist you in understanding certain nonverbal clues.

- **Analyze the appearance of the face**: If a person can maintain eye contact during the conversation, Observe where they are looking to discover whether or not they find the talk interesting. You can also tell whether someone is surprised or interested by the movement of their eyebrows.
- **Pay attention to the lips and jaw:** Pay attention to the lips and jaw for any possible indicators of discontent as well as evidence that they are

happy or engaged in the conversation.

- **Conduct a review of the posture and gestures:** There are signals that you may be creating a solid relationship with your listener if they are sitting near to you or moving closer to you while you speak. Sincerity may be communicated by open hands or arms. The fact that your listener is mirroring your behaviors is another possible indication that you have their attention.

- **Pay attention to your tone of speech:** How a person speaks might also give away their emotions. The ability to maintain a consistent rhythm may convey assurance and readiness. 5. Investigate potential parallels. To accurately understand someone's body language, one of the most important steps is to seek several indications. For instance, if you pay attention to a person's nonverbal cues, you may be able to distinguish between someone who is concentrating and someone who is astonished.

# Chapter 2

## Having a good understanding of nonverbal communication (Body Language)

The term "body language" refers to the nonverbal cues that humans utilize to communicate with one another. These nonverbal cues are an essential component of regular conversation and interaction. Expressions on one's face, where one directs one's gaze, gestures, posture, and other bodily motions are all examples of body language. In many situations, the things that we do not say might convey a significant amount of information. There are so many ways to understand humans and their intentions.

## Expressions on the Face

Consider for a second how much information can be sent just via a person's choice of facial expression. A grin may convey a variety of emotions, including approbation and enjoyment. The expression of disapproval or dissatisfaction may be conveyed by frowning. There are times when the looks on our faces may tell others exactly how we are feeling about a certain circumstance. Even when you report that you are feeling well, others may be able to tell by the expression on your face that this is not the case. Many other feelings may be communicated by facial expressions, including happiness, anger, surprise, disgust, fear, desire, and contempt to name just a few. There is joy, confusion, excitement, desire, and disdain all rolled into one. What someone is saying may even be used to assist in assessing whether or not we trust or believe what that person is saying just by seeing the look on their face.

In the field of psychology, there have been many fascinating discoveries made concerning body language. According to the findings of one research, the most trustworthy facial expression is characterized by a very tiny upward movement of the eyebrows and a very slight grin. According to the findings of the study, this face communicates not just friendliness but also assurance.

**The Eyes**

The Eyes are sometimes referred to as the "windows to the Soul" because they are capable of expressing a great deal about what a person is feeling or thinking, which is why they are commonly given this nickname. Observing the other person's eye movements when you are discussing with them is a natural and essential component of the communication process. If individuals are making direct eye contact with you or if they are avoiding their gaze, how often they are blinking, and whether or not their pupils are dilated are all factors that are likely to come to your attention. Paying attention is the most effective strategy for interpreting the body language of another person. Keep an eye out for any of the following potential eye indications.

- When someone stares straight into your eyes while you are having a discussion, it is a sign that they are interested in what you are saying and paying attention to what you are saying. However, sustained eye contact might give the impression of hostility. On the other side, avoiding eye contact and glancing away often may be signs that the person is preoccupied, uncomfortable, or attempting to disguise his or her true sentiments.

- Blinking is a completely normal bodily function, but you should nevertheless pay attention to whether or not a person is blinking excessively or insufficiently. When someone is anxious or otherwise uncomfortable, they often blink more quickly than normal. If a person blinks very seldom, it may be a sign that they are consciously making an effort to regulate the movement of their eyes.

- The size of one's pupils may be a very subtle indicator of nonverbal communication. Pupil dilation is mostly controlled by the amounts of light in the surrounding environment; however, occasionally feelings may also induce little variations in pupil size. Dilated eyes, for instance, might indicate that a person is intrigued or even aroused.

You may have heard the expression "bedroom eyes" used to describe the look someone has when they are attracted to somebody individual.

## The Mouth

The oral cavity Reading body language also requires paying attention to the emotions and movements of the mouth. For instance, if a person is chewing on their bottom lip, it may be a sign that they are experiencing negative emotions such as anxiety, fear, or insecurity. If the individual is yawning or coughing, covering the mouth may be an attempt to be courteous, but it may also be an attempt to hide up a scowl of displeasure. Smiling is perhaps one of the most effective body language cues, but smiles may also be understood in a variety of other contexts. A grin can be genuine, but it is also possible for it to be employed to convey fake delight, sarcasm, or even cynicism.

When analyzing body language, it is important to pay attention to the following mouth and lip signals:

- **Pursed lips**: Lips that are tightly pursed might be seen as a sign of disgust, rejection, or mistrust.
- **Chewing on the lower lip**: When frightened, apprehensive, or upset, some people may unconsciously bite the inside of their lips.
- **The mouth is being covered:** People may sometimes cover their lips to prevent grins or smirks when they are trying to conceal an emotional response. This is because smiling or smirking might give away their true feelings. Either turned up or turned down.
- Alterations in a person's lips, even minute ones, may sometimes be used as covert markers of what they are experiencing. When a person's lips are tilted up ever so slightly, it may be an indication that they are feeling

joyful or hopeful. On the other hand, a mouth that is tilted slightly downward might be interpreted as a sign of melancholy, displeasure, or even a full-blown grimace.

## The Hand Motions

Hand motions Body language signals may be quite plain and evident, and gestures are often included in this category. Indicating numerical quantities by waving one's hand, pointing one's finger, or utilizing one's fingers are all extremely typical motions that are simple to interpret. However, certain gestures may have cultural connotations; for example, in some countries, giving the middle finger or making the peace sign may have an entirely different significance than they do in the United States. The examples that follow are only a few instances of frequent gestures and their various meanings:

- A clenched fist may signify anger in some circumstances, but in other circumstances, it might show unity.
- The motions of giving the thumbs up or down are often employed to express appreciation or displeasure, respectively.
- The "okay" gesture, which is created by touching together the thumb and index finger in a circle while extending the other three fingers, can be used to mean "okay" or "all right."
- The "V" sign, which is created by lifting the index and middle finger and separating them to create a V-shape, can mean peace or victory in some countries.

**The Arms and Legs**

The arms and legs are equally important nonverbal communication tools. Arms that are crossed over one another may be a sign of defensiveness. The act of crossing one's legs away from another person may be seen as a sign of distaste or discomfort with that person. Keeping the arms near to the body may be an effort to shrink oneself or retreat from attention while stretching the arms broadly may be an attempt to look bigger or more authoritative. Other subtle signals, such as expanding the arms widely, may also be used.

When analyzing body language, it is important to pay attention to the many messages that may be sent by the arms and legs. One of these indications is that a person may feel defensive, self-protective, or walled off if they have their arms crossed.

- When a person stands with their hands on their hips, it might be an indicator that they are ready and in control, but it can also potentially be a clue that they are aggressive.
- The act of clasping one's hands behind one's back may be interpreted

as a sign that the individual is feeling bored, uncomfortable, or even furious.

- Fidgeting or tapping one's fingers quickly in rapid succession may be a symptom that a person is bored, irritable, or irritated.
- When a person crosses their legs, it may be a sign that they are feeling closed off or that they need privacy.

## Standing stance

How we hold our bodies may also be a significant component of our body language. When we talk about someone's posture, we're talking about how they hold their bodies in general, as well as their entire physical shape.

A person's posture may provide a variety of information about how they are feeling as well as suggestions about the features of their personality, such as whether or not they are confident, open, or subservient.

For example, if a person is sitting up straight, it may be an indication that they are attentive and paying attention to what is going on around them. On the other hand, sitting with the body bent forward might give the impression that the individual is either bored or uninterested in the situation. When you are attempting to interpret body language, one of the signals that a person's posture might transmit is how they are standing or sitting.

- Maintaining an open posture requires maintaining the front and sides of the body exposed and open. This stance conveys friendliness, openness, and willingness on the part of the person adopting it.
- A closed posture is one in which the trunk of the body is obscured, often by slouching forward and maintaining a crossing position of the arms and legs. This particular position may be seen as an indication

of animosity, unfriendliness, or nervousness.

## Proxemics

Have you ever heard someone talk about how they need a certain amount of privacy for themselves? Have you ever gotten to the point where someone standing just a little bit too close to you made you feel uncomfortable? The study of the distance that exists between individuals throughout interaction is known as proxemics. The amount of physical distance that exists between two people may convey a considerable lot of information even if they do not speak the same language. This is true of both facial expressions and body language. Four distinct tiers of social distance may be found in various settings.

- **Intimate Distance:** This amount of physical distance often denotes a tighter connection or a higher level of comfort between persons. It most often takes place during close physical contact, such as when two people are embracing, speaking, or caressing one another.

- **Personal Distance**: This is the term used to describe the physical distance that exists between persons who are either members of the same family or very close friends. The amount of closeness in a couple's relationship may be gauged by how near they can stand to one another while maintaining their comfort.
- **Social Distance:** The term "social distance" refers to the physical distance that exists between two people who are already acquainted with one another.
- **Public Distance:** The term "public distance" refers to a physical distance at this level, which is often employed in circumstances involving public speaking. Examples of such circumstances include delivering a

presentation in front of one's coworkers or front of an entire classroom full of pupils.

## What Roles Do Nonverbal Forms of Communication Play in Social Interaction?

Body language plays a variety of important functions in social interactions,. The following are some of the things that it may assist facilitate:

1. Developing trust involves making eye contact with another person, nodding your head in agreement while they are speaking, and even subconsciously mimicking their body language. All of these behaviors are signs that you and the other person are connecting.

2. The tone of your voice, the way you engage your audience with your hand and arm motions, and the amount of space you take up all have

an impact on how your message is received.

3. When someone's body language does not match what they are saying, we may instinctively pick up on the idea that they are hiding information or possibly not being honest about how they feel. This can be a sign that they are lying about how they feel about something.

4. Learning to read your body language may tell us a lot about how we're feeling, therefore it's important to become attuned to your requirements. For example, do you have a slouched posture, tighten your jaw, or pursed your lips when you feel stressed? This might be a clue that the setting in which you now find yourself is causing you to experience triggers in some manner. Your body may be trying to communicate with you that it senses danger, worry, or any other variety

of feelings. However, it is important to keep in mind that your interpretations of the meanings sent by the body language of others may not always be correct.

# Chapter 3

## The Driving Force Behind People's Action

People's actions may be explained by a collection of needs that we refer to as motivational factors or motivations or driving force. These requirements fall into three categories: organic motivators, social motivators, and psychological motivators. Let's speak about what motivates us in the first place, the motivational factors. The cues that motivate a person to take particular behaviors, which demand an effort to reach an aim, are what we refer to as the motivational factors.

Our degree of strain is the maximum treasured asset we own. Its worth is determined by action, and it varies depending on how we engage our attention in it. There are biological underpinnings to some of our reasons for acting, while other reasons have more personal or societal roots. We are driven to seek out food, water, and sex; but, our conduct is also impacted by social approval and acceptability, the urge to accomplish, and the motivation to either take risks or avoid them, to mention just a few of these influences.

## Various Forms of Motivation

One's internal drive might serve as a source of motivation. Biological variables are those that are generated in a person's brain and neurological system, while psychological variables are those that indicate qualities of a person's thinking, such as psychological requirements. It is common practice to think of environmental factors, such as incentives or objectives when referring to the sources of motivation that come from the outside.

The combination of our internal and external sources of motivation is what ultimately directs our conduct. Our evolutionary past may also shed light on some elements of motivation and behavior, while the unique narratives of each of our lives help form our motivations and establish the extent to which certain objectives and incentives are useful. These are various forms of motivation.

## Encouragement and Push

The production of epinephrine and norepinephrine by the sympathetic nervous system results in the generation of action-oriented energy.This may be the motive why humans normally have a tendency to consider motivation in terms of drives. Our bodies constantly work toward achieving a desirable end-state and diminishing or getting rid of the urge to achieve it. This is known as homeostasis. The internal motivations that excite, guide, and maintain conduct are referred to as needs. They give rise to the kinds of aspirations that are essential to the preservation of life, development, and well-being.

Physiological wishes are the organic origins that in the end screen themselves as mental impulses. These physiological needs encompass such things as hunger, thirst, sex, and so on. These organic occurrences subsequently become mental motivations. It is critical to make a distinction between the physiological need and the psychological desire that it produces since only the latter has features that can be described as motivating. According to the power principle of motivation, the inspiration of our motivation lies withinside the physiological needs of our bodies. When our body's physiological system makes an effort to preserve our health, it generates psychological drive and drives us to move the system from a state of insufficiency toward a state of equilibrium.

## The Drive to Achieve Goals

When discussing what motivates people, the subject of objectives will certainly be brought up. A goal is a cognitive mental event that operates like a "spring to action" by energizing and directing our behavior in meaningful ways and motivating others to behave in diverse ways. Goals are a source of internal motivation, much as a person's attitude, beliefs, expectations, and self-concept.

These intellectual assets of motivation paintings collectively to energise us and spur us into action. That which does not exist, or, said another way, the gap between where we are and where we aspire to be, is the seed from which goals are grown. The proverb "If you don't know where you're going, any road will get you there" explains the difference in motivated behavior between those who have objectives and others who do not have goals.

However, just formulating objectives is not always instructive in and of itself. Setting goals may be a motivating construct; but, for this to convert into performance, the objectives themselves need to be hard, precise, and compatible with the individual.

**Inspiration and Emotional State**
Both the words motivation and emotion originate from the same Latin root,

"movere" which can be translated as "to move". Emotions are taken into consideration to be states of motivation due to the fact they generate bursts of energy that get our interest and motivate our reactions to splendid activities in our lives.

The drive to find a way to deal with one's current situation is prompted by one's feelings. Affect is the umbrella term for a basic set of psychological phenomena that includes both emotion and motivation as parts. We sense those sensations, each bodily and emotionally, and that they encourage and have an impact on our conduct and decision-making. Perhaps most significantly, these experiences have a profound effect on both our mental and physical health.

**Personality and motivational factor**
Personality qualities influence how we are driven to varying degrees. We will be

more open to experience, conscientious, extraverted, pleasant, and neurotic if we have a high level of a certain attribute, and we will also behave as the trait suggests if we have a high degree of that feature. Not only will we be inspired by a variety of activities, objectives, and rewards, but we will also consciously put ourselves in a variety of predicaments.

## Encouragement Towards Change

In the context of transition, the subject of motivation is regularly brought up for discussion. The process of transformation is seldom either straightforward or straightforward. One of the reasons for this is that it may be difficult to find the desire to participate in activities that are not inherently cross and gain carry for microscale stimulating, and this is a factor that contributes to the problem. On the surface, many shifts seem to be bad; nevertheless, you will quickly understand that these shifts are making room in your life for something new to emerge. The readiness for change, which is defined by our willingness to change, confidence in our ability to bring about the desired change, and actions done to bring about the desired change, works hand in hand with increasing motivation.

Understanding the ideas of motivation allows us to discover achievable answers to real-global motivational problems. What could be more essential than enabling individuals in our immediate environment to take more deliberate actions, realize their goals, have the best possible experiences, fully function, grow healthily, and have a strong sense of who they are?

The study of motivational science and its practical application may also assist us in overcoming impulsive drives, habitual experiences, the inability to achieve goals, unproductive functioning, unpleasant emotions, boredom, maladaptive or dysfunctional growth, and a fragile sense of self.

# Chapter 4

## Personality and Psychological Profiling

The term "personality type" comes from the field of psychology and relates to the psychological categorization of distinct sorts of people. There is a distinction that can be made between personality types and personality characteristics, with the latter representing a more narrowly defined cluster of behavioral inclinations. People are frequently said to vary from one another in a qualitative rather than a quantitative manner, which is why types and characteristics are often contrasted with one another. People who are classified as introverts and those who are classified as extroverts, for instance, are said to belong to two fundamentally distinct kinds of individuals, according to type theories. Many individuals fall somewhere in the center of the continuum between introversion and extraversion, which is consistent with the predictions of trait theories.

In contrast to the effect that stereotyping has, which is to reduce one's level of knowledge and understanding of persons, effective personality typologies shed light on individuals and lead to a deeper comprehension of who they are. successful typologies also provide for enhanced capacity to forecast clinically important facts about persons and to build successful treatment methods. There is a wealth of published material on the subject of categorizing the many kinds of human temperament, and there is an equally vast body of published material on the subject of personality characteristics or domains. These categorization systems make an effort to characterize normal temperament and personality while highlighting the defining characteristics of various temperament and personality types; they are primarily the purview of the academic field of psychology. On the other hand, personality disorders are disease-oriented and mirror the work that is done in the field of psychiatry, which is a branch of medicine.

## The Five Major Categories of Personality.

What are the top five characteristics that define a person's personality? This has turned out to be an unexpectedly demanding undertaking, and the fact that not all characteristics of personality are created equal adds another layer of complexity to the situation. Some characteristics are more important than others when it comes to understanding people's behaviors and predicting important outcomes in people's lives. These outcomes include

- The nature of people's relationships with others
- The degree to which they are successful at achieving their goals
- Their psychological well-being, and
- Their health.

A large majority of people concluded that the human personality can be broken down into five fundamental characteristics. These 5 traits had been together stated as "The Big Five," and that they had been the issue of an giant quantity of study. There are a great number of additional characteristics, but these five have been identified as being the most essential for comprehending the personalities and actions of other individuals. But before we get into these five characteristics, let's first define precisely what we mean when we talk about personality traits.

## What precisely is a "Personality Trait"?

A person's inclination to react in a certain manner is an example of a personality feature. Personality traits are internal, psychological characteristics. Consider your behavior: In the presence of new people, do you have a reputation for being extroverted or more reserved? You are possibly neither of these matters all of the time; at times, you're possibly extra extroverted, and at different times, you're possibly extra reserved. However, if we were to follow you and see how you behaved in a variety of settings, we would most likely discover that you had a bias toward one particular direction or the other. You may also have a tendency to be greater extroverted, even as it is also viable which you have a tendency to be greater reserved. You might also additionally have a few mental trait, or possibly a hard and fast of traits, that predisposes you to react in a single manner or another. As a result, we'd say which you have a trait that predisposes you to have a tendency to be outgoing, reserved, or some thing else.

The reality which you display a specific tendency in the way you reply throughout conditions shows which you possess few mental characteristic, or possibly a hard and fast of characteristics, that predisposes you to react in a single manner or another. A person is said to exhibit a particular degree of consistency in their ideas, emotions, or actions regardless of the context in which they find themselves since this is what the notion of a characteristic entails according to its definition. If you have a specific attribute, then we should be able to recognize a pattern in which you behave in a particular manner regardless of the context in which you find yourself. Even though a person has a characteristic, it does not mean that they will always behave in the same manner.

People who consistently behave in the same manner are unable to adjust their actions to meet the requirements of the many contexts in which they find themselves. No matter how outgoing you are, there will be moments when you need to be reserved. Likewise, no matter how reserved you typically are, there will be occasions when circumstances force you to be social. Therefore, the idea of a characteristic in no way suggests that a person always behaves in the same manner; such consistency in behavior would be indicative of a personality disorder. To reiterate, possessing a characteristic only denotes that individuals have a propensity to react in a specific manner. Personality characteristics may and can change with time, at least within certain bounds, although this is not always the case. In the near term, however, we see consistency in their characteristics. If you have been more outgoing than usual this month, it is not probable that we will discover that you have grown more reserved over the next several months.

Now let's discuss about the five most prominent characteristics of a person's personality. The Big Five Model, sometimes referred to as the Five-Factor Model, is currently the theory of personality that has the greatest level of acceptance among psychologists. According to this idea, an individual's personality may be broken down into five primary components, also referred to by the acronyms CANOE and OCEAN. The following are the Big Five character traits:

## 1. Openness

Out of the five personality qualities, openness (also known as openness to experience) stresses imagination and insight the most. People with a excessive stage of openness generally tend to have a various set of interests. They are curious about the sector and different people, and they're geared up to analyze new matters and feature new experiences. People with a immoderate diploma of this man or woman trait are also more ambitious and innovative.People who rating low in this character function have a tendency to be extra conventional and can battle with summary thinking.

High

- Very inventive.
- Open to new experiences.
- Dedicated to taking over new challenges.

- Enjoy thinking about abstract concepts.

Low.

- Dislikes shift.
- Doesn't like attempting new things.
- New ideas are met with hostility.
- Not very creative.
- Dislikes summary or theoretical concepts

## 2. Conscientiousness

Conscientiousness is an individual feature characterized via immoderate degrees of thinking, pinnacle impulse control, and goal-directed behaviors. Highly conscientious people are installed and detail-oriented.They plan in advance of time, bear in mind how their moves have an effect on others, and preserve time limits in mind. Someone with a lower score on this key personality attribute is less ordered and orderly. They may postpone to finish tasks, sometimes entirely missing deadlines.

High.

- Spends time planning.
- Completes critical responsibilities quickly.
- Pays near interest to details.
- He likes having a defined schedule.

Low.

- Structure and schedules irritate him.
- Makes messes and is careless with stuff.
- Failure to return items or place them where they belong.

- They puts off crucial responsibilities.
- Failure to fulfill required or assigned responsibilities.

## 3. Extraversion

Extraversion (moreover known as extroversion) is a personality function that is characterized via excitability, friendliness, talkativeness, assertiveness, and a immoderate diploma of emotional expressiveness. Extraverts are gregarious and will be predisposed to gain strength in social situations. Being in the company of others makes them feel invigorated and excited. People who're introverted or have a low degree of this personality trait are extra reserved. They have an awful lot power to expend in social

situations, and social gatherings can be exhausting. Introverts often require silence to "recharge."
High.

- Takes pleasure in being the focus of attention.
- Likes to strike up talks.
- They like meeting new folks.
- Has a massive social circle of associates and friends.
- It is simple for them to meet new pals.
- When they are around other people, they feel energized.
- They something before they think about it.

Low

- Prefers to be alone.
- Feels fatigued when forced to mingle frequently.

- It is tough for them to strike up a discussion.
- They dislikes small conversations.
- Before speaking, they carefully consider their options.
- They dislikes being the point of interest of attention

## 4. Agreeableness

Trust, benevolence, friendliness, affection, and different prosocial acts are examples of this persona feature. People with immoderate agreeableness will be inclined to be extra cooperative, even as human beings with low agreeableness will be inclined to be extra competitive, and every now and then even manipulative.

High.

- Has a strong interest in other people.
- Concerned about others.
- Feels compassion and empathy towards others.
- Enjoys assisting others and contributing to their happiness.
- Assists others who need assistance

Low.

- Has scant regard for others.
- Doesn't give a damn about how other people feel.
- Is uninterested in other people's concerns.
- Insults and dismisses others.
- Manipulates others to achieve their goals.

## 5. Neuroticism

Sadness, moodiness, and emotional instability are trends of neuroticism.Individuals with excessive neuroticism are vulnerable to temper fluctuations, anxiety, impatience, and unhappiness.Those with low stages of this personality trait are more strong and emotionally resilient.

High.

- Has a immoderate degree of stress.
- Worries about a variety of issues.
- Is easily agitated.
- Dramatic mood swings occur.
- Has a nervous feeling.
- Struggles to recover from traumatic circumstances.

Low

- Emotionally sound.

- Handles stress well.
- He is rarely melancholy or depressed.
- It's not a big deal.
- Is very laid-back

The Big Five stay reasonably steady over much of one's existence. They are impacted considerably by genes and the environment. They also predict some critical life outcomes like education and health. Each attribute reflects a continuum. Individuals may fall anywhere on the spectrum for each attribute. Unlike other characteristic theories that categorize people into binary groups (i.e. introvert or extrovert ), the Big Five Model maintains that each personality attribute is a continuum. Therefore, people are graded on a scale between the two extreme ends of five broad dimensions.

# Conclusion

One of the most crucial things you can know is how to read people. It makes you sensitive to the challenges and wants of the people around you. It is a talent that you may master to further increase your EQ. The good news is that anybody can read people. The fact of the matter is that all you need is the knowledge to know what to search for.